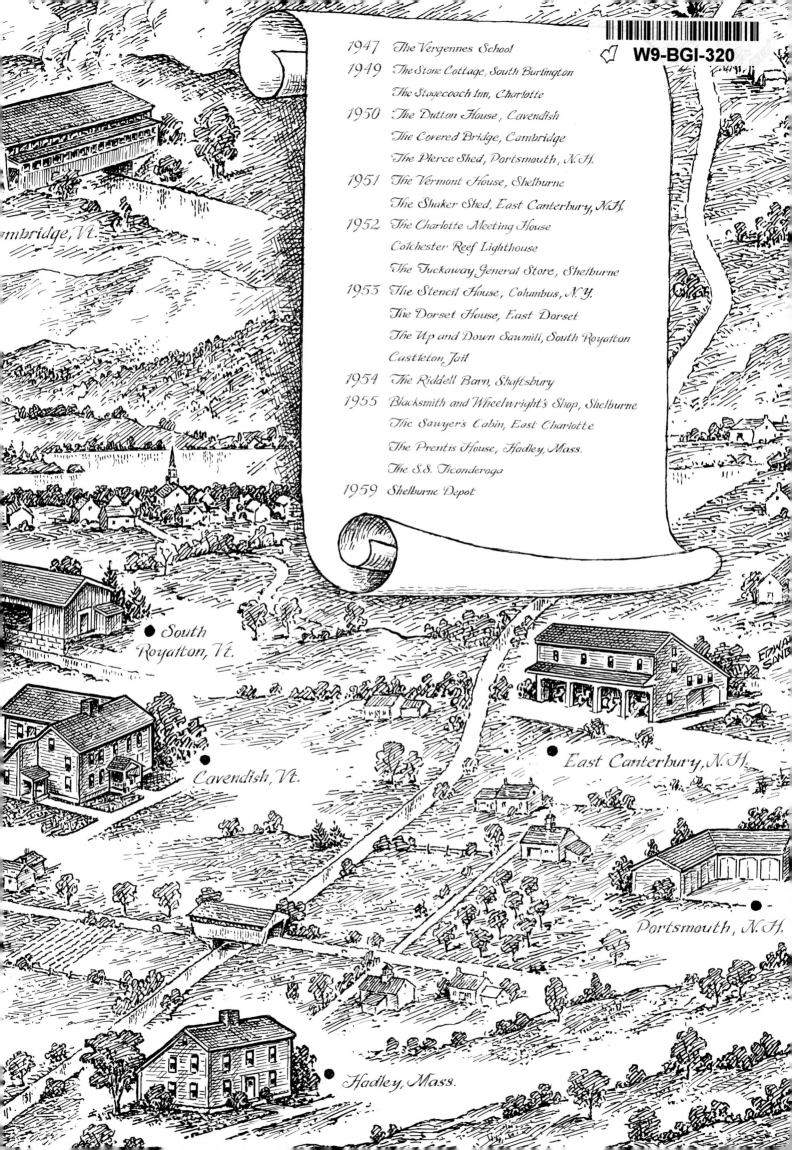

Cambridge, Vt.

South Royalton, Vt.

Cavendish, Vt.

East Canterbury, N.H.

Portsmouth, N.H.

Hadley, Mass.

"Art [will] hold up her head and say: 'I am a first necessity; all else may be cheap, but I shall ever be in demand. My present owner's fortune may crumble, his title may vanish, his manhood deteriorate, but I shall survive and with proud prestige of fame, passion from generation to generation, from one great land to another, bearing regardless of race or time my message unto all mankind.' "

A
Pictorial History
of the
Shelburne Museum

RICHARD LAWRENCE GREENE

AND

KENNETH EDWARD WHEELING

The Shelburne Museum
Shelburne, Vermont

MCMLXXII

THE SHELBURNE MUSEUM

INCORPORATED

J. WATSON WEBB, Jr.
Chairman of the Board

SAMUEL B. WEBB, JR.
President

BRIAN ALEXANDER
Director

This book is one of a series on early American arts
and antiques published by the museum. For a list
of these publications, write directly to
the Shelburne Museum, Shelburne, Vermont 05482

Copyright © 1972, by the Shelburne Museum, Inc., Shelburne, Vermont.
First printing, Burlington, Vermont 1972
Second printing, Burlington, Vermont 1982
Third, revised printing, Burlington, Vermont 1988
Cover design by Eugenie Seidenberg

ISBN 0-939384-04-3

TABLE OF CONTENTS

FOREWORD

In 1946, right after World War II, Mother, Electra Havemeyer Webb, first thought about starting a Museum in which she wanted to place for exhibit to the public many of her treasures which she had collected ever since her marriage to Father, James Watson Webb, in 1910. Soon after she had the idea, Uncle Vanderbilt Webb offered her the Webb family collection of carriages which had been preserved on Shelburne Farms in the Coach Barn. In 1947, the Shelburne Museum was founded by Mother and Father and plans to exhibit her "Collection of Collections" and the Webb carriages were started. From 1947 until 1960, Mother, always with Father's encouragement, never stopped forging ahead with her dream to contribute something worthwhile to our American heritage.

On October 1, 1960, while still in perfect health, and while visiting Stowe with her faithful friend, Duncan Munro, Mother collapsed as the result of a stroke. For six and a half weeks, she clung to life by a thread while her children gathered at her side, always hoping for the best. Suddenly after all those weeks of unconsciousness she "awoke" and made perfect sense. We all enjoyed a few happy days together with her in her hospital room. On the night of November 18, 1960, her children and her oldest friend, Georgie W. Rathborne, were at her bedside, and as we said good night to her we all commented on what a remarkable recovery she was making. Not once but twice she said to all of us: "If you think I've done well today, wait till you see the way I'm going to *Forge Ahead* tomorrow!" In the early hours of November 19, she had another stroke and died without saying another word. The last words I heard her say, "forge ahead," were so indelibly imprinted in my mind that, as soon as I took over the reins of the Shelburne Museum, I decided to use those words as our motto.

Above the entrance to the Webb Art Gallery hangs an American wooden eagle which Mother collected years and years ago and which for many, many years hung in the high-ceilinged living room in our home in Westbury, Long Island. I decided that I would use that eagle — since the eagle is symbolic of America — as our emblem and into its talons I had drawn a banner on which I put the words *Forge Ahead*. That is why I have chosen this eagle for the cover of our 25th Anniversary *A Pictorial History of the Shelburne Museum*. In Mother's 13 years at the helm of the Museum, she never stopped forging ahead. Since her death in 1960, we have continued to try and do the same — and always will.

DEDICATION

This book is dedicated to ALL the employees of the Shelburne Museum, both past and present, as without them and without their interest, and their enthusiasm, and their loyalty, and their devotion, and their dedication, there would be no Museum the way one sees it today. To all those friends, I extend my sincere and heartfelt and appreciative thanks, and I extend special thanks to Kenneth Wheeling and to Richard Greene for their tireless efforts while putting together this book for me. I also want to express my grateful thanks to the many photographers who have taken the thousands of excellent photographs of the Museum from its inception till today and from which photographs we have selected the "best of Shelburne" for this book on our *Pictorial History*.

This book is also dedicated to the following friends of the Shelburne Museum without whose generous contributions publication of this book would not have been possible.

Dunbar W. Bostwick Foundation
Laura W. and Archibald M. Brown, Jr.
Dundeen B. and Daniel Catlin, Jr.
Gloria S. and Wilfrid A. Daly, Jr.
J. Richardson Dilworth
Marion and Sterling D. Emerson
George G. Frelinghuysen
Esmé O'B. Hammond
James H. Maroney, Jr.
John Mayer
Electra B. and Fletcher McDowell
Eleanor L. Nowlin
Georgie W. Rathborne
Rebecca and Louis J. Wainer
Elizabeth C. and Derick V. Webb
Martha T. and Samuel B. Webb
Harry H. Webb
Julie D. and Samuel B. Webb, Jr.
Kate B. Webb

J. Watson Webb, Jr.
Chairman of the Board

A MUSEUM COMES TO SHELBURNE

No stranger to activity, Shelburne, Vermont, has experienced quite a number of startling events. Long before Governor Benning Wentworth gave the town its charter in 1763, the moccasins of Indian warriors trampled the grass along the east side of Lake Champlain. Soon after settlement, strange looking lumber rafts were floating north, and scows, loaded with potash, headed down the lake to Montreal. Proudly named for the English earl who defended the Hampshire grants against the claims of the Yorkers, the settlement was almost deserted during the Revolution of 1776. Southern Vermont offered greater security against the Indian attacks incited by the Tory Loyalists. During the War of 1812, Lieutenant Macdonough quartered his men in Shelburne homes. Soon thereafter, the sheltered bay on the west side of the township grew used to the sounds of sidewheelers coming and going to their shipyard home.

It was just another day when Mrs. J. Watson Webb purchased the first land whereon to build her museum in 1947. The sequel was cause for at least astonishment, perhaps even sharp Yankee wit. Three buildings in the town were moved right off their foundations and onto the museum property. Up the main thoroughfare of the village came building after building. Perhaps, then, no one here was really surprised when they found out that she was going to have a 900 ton steamboat hauled through the woods to the museum. Generations to come will enjoy the tales that are told about the time a museum came to Shelburne.

Locating buildings for Shelburne Museum was hardly a problem. Scouting the countryside for likely additions was one of Electra Webb's favorite pastimes, and in the late 1940's and early 50's, there were still many to be found. Hundreds of old barns, shops, and houses lay hidden along Vermont's back roads and country lanes, vacant and declining in a state of picturesque decrepitude. Once they had been scenes of life and activity, but now they stood silent except for the echoing footfalls of an occasional curious visitor. For an elect few of these buildings on the brink of oblivion, the future would bring rebirth and a new life in idyllic surroundings.

The Dorset House as it appeared in 1953

The Dutton House awaiting removal at Cavendish, Vermont

The Stage Coach Inn, Charlotte, Vermont

Attic of the Dorset House during dismantling. Roofing has been removed, allowing light to shine through the hand-split lath.

8

Dismantling the Dutton House, Cavendish, Vermont. Interior panelling and floor boards removed, the roof, clapboards, boarding and frame followed. Carrying partitions, where they existed, came down with the frame as did the chimney.

The Diamond Barn from Shaftsbury, Vermont. Roofing and clapboarding removed, the unusual frame is well displayed.

Brick by brick the walls of the Charlotte Meeting House grow smaller. Stripped of its roofing, the hand-hewn beams of the framework stand open to the sky.

9

Occasionally a building would be close enough to the museum or small enough to be moved almost intact. Such was the case with the Tuckaway General Store. For a quarter of a mile, it inched through Shelburne over specially laid tracks.

Raising the ridgepole of the Diamond Barn, a re-enactment of its own beginnings.

Removed from its original site and shorn of rustic nostalgia, a building at the halfway point is a lonely, desolate entity.

When restored and landscaped, it becomes that rare and comely beauty called a home. So it is with this Dutton House. So it will be with others.

THE COVERED BRIDGE

Long before the days of structural steel, men devised ways to bridge a river. They used either stone or wood, or a combination thereof, and they employed one or another engineering technique to increase the load capabilities. With their particular ingenuity for distinctive architecture, the Americans spanned many streams and rivers with covered bridges. Almost divinized, examples of such bridges are highly prized and eagerly studied. They draw a wide audience among travelers.

In 1845, a covered bridge was built across the Lamoille River at Cambridge, Vermont, complete with footpath and double lane. In 1949, the Vermont Department of Highways decided to replace what one hundred years of work and weather had failed to destroy. They gave the bridge to Shelburne Museum.

The bridge was uniquely suited to the museum's purposes. Employing a design patented by Theodore Burr in 1804, it was a superb addition to the little collection of buildings at Shelburne. Great arches, strengthened by a series of multiple king-post braces and counterbraces, soared from one abutment to the other. From end to end, it was 168 feet long.

11

Dismantling the bridge was difficult. Every beam and brace was pegged in place with stout wooden trunnels. But, one by one, each piece came out of its place, numbered beforehand for reassembly. As work went relentlessly on, the ribs of this great giant slowly dwindled in number as the trucks carried them south to the museum.

The problem of placement was solved with the suggestion that it become the entrance to the museum. A small pond was dug to provide a pleasing, as well as plausible, setting for the bridge, and again people wend their way across, this time to the world from which the bridge came.

"We crossed the river by a wooden bridge, roofed and covered on all sides, and nearly a mile in length. It was profoundly dark; perplexed with great beams, crossing and recrossing it at every possible angle; and through the broad chinks and crevices in the floor, the rapid river gleamed, far down below, like a legion of eyes."

Charles Dickens

THE VARIETY UNIT

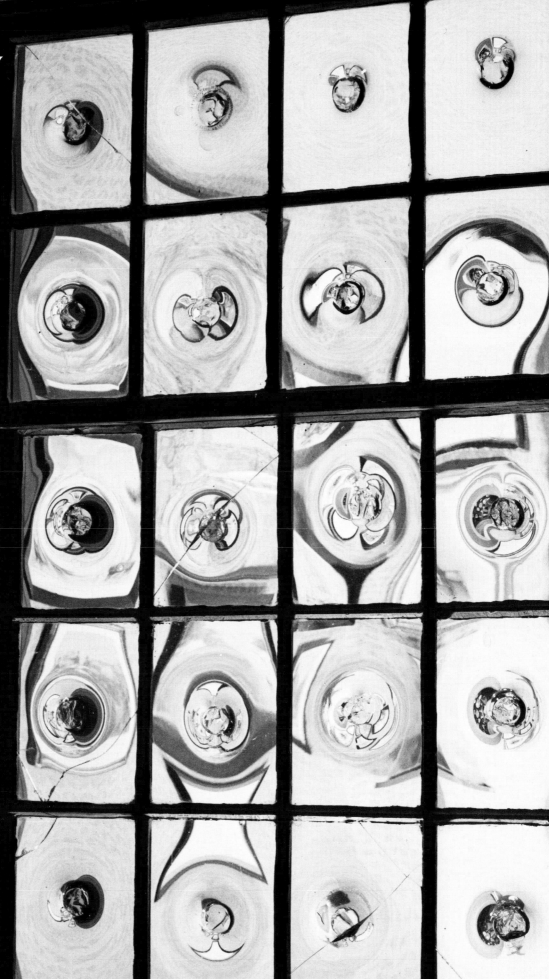

As the light swirls and writhes around the bull's eye panes . . .

. . . creating a limitless variety of patterns, so an endless series of nooks and niches create a fantasyland where glassware and china sparkle on their shelves and a visitor's disbelief is reflected in the polished pewter.

Shelburne Museum began when it took ownership of an eight-acre piece of ground and a red brick dwelling known as the Weed House. The brick structure was built around 1840 and added to a wooden shed of sorts which had been built sometime earlier. Though the ell was enlarged and closed in, the entire unit is the only building at the museum on its original site. Undergoing many changes during the formative period of museum growth, it finally emerged as The Variety Unit. Downstairs, various galleries and rooms house specialty collections, while upstairs, shuttered windows mask the small, small world of almost fifteen hundred dolls.

Pewter nursing bottle
Probably American
Date unknown

Photo by C. Robert Callahan

Pewter was a seventeenth century luxury which only a few could afford. Imported by the shipload, English pewter quickly disappeared into the homes of affluent colonists. Although demand was high, American pewterers were hampered by the English tariff on raw tin. Even when pewter became plentiful, a farmhouse could boast of no more than one or two plates and a few spoons. This curious combination of tin, copper and lead could easily be hammered, turned or cast into a variety of domestic utensils and even into refined tea sets and communion services. A representative collection of continental pewter is displayed in the Pewter Room of the Variety Unit.

Tucked away in this petite and finely-crafted room is a collection of figure jugs. For 600 years, the English have served their drinks in these ceramic toby jugs, and many a tippler has found himself immortalized beneath the potter's glaze. Gigantic jugs, sitting about the floor, seem to dwarf the lustre pitchers on the shelves above. The Duke of Wellington graces the side of one of these Staffordshire trade signs, this one commemorating Waterloo, 1815.

Leaving the Toby Room, the visitor is confronted by battalions of teapots — shelf after shelf of them, of every shape and size: Staffordshire, Whieldon, Worcester, Chelsea, Crown Derby. . . .

Tea is a gift to the west from China, but no one has made it so popular as the English who marketed the serving ware for it as well. Their business acumen was extraordinary, as this particular teapot attests. Made by the English firm of Enoch Wood and Sons for the American market, it depicts Macdonough's defeat of the British on Lake Champlain in 1814.

The Macdonough Room

Threading one's way through the passages of the Variety Unit, the visitor turns a corner and finds himself surrounded by mementos of the days during the War of 1812 when Lake Champlain was the scene of a Naval engagement as fierce as any on the high seas. The Battle of Plattsburgh, on September 18, 1814, ended, decisively, the threat of a British invasion from Canada, and the results were clearly reflected in the treaty of Ghent which ended the war. Hero of the battle was the victorious Lieutenant Thomas Macdonough, whose accomplishments are celebrated in the prints, paintings, maps and engravings displayed in this room named in his honor.

Porcelain plate in the pattern of the Society of Cincinnati, the fraternal veterans organization of which Macdonough was a member

Commodore Thomas Macdonough

Tylers Farm, Lake Champlain, 1813. This sketch apparently depicts Macdonough's fleet a year prior to the battle.

Late 19th Century steel engraving of Macdonough's victory

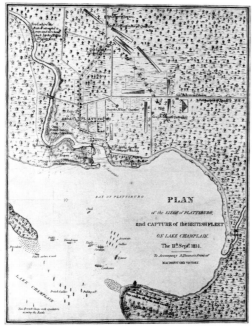

"Time . . . devourer of all things"
Ovid

With a history almost as intricate as the clocks themselves, American clockmakers were no laggards among colonial craftsmen. The Willards of Massachusetts were busily marketing their clocks three years before the colonies severed themselves from England.

Scrimshaw pocket sundial;
Brass ring-dial

Three men from Connecticut revolutionized clockmaking by complacently shifting from brass movements to wood and back to brass if convenient. Eli Terry, responsible for the Pillar and Scroll Shelf Clock above, started business in 1793 at Northbury. He manufactured an inexpensive clock with wooden parts. Silas Hoadley and Seth Thomas, apprentices in Terry's second factory at Plymouth, bought him out, were partners for a time, and then went into business separately. The museum's Clock Room unfolds the tale of these changing relationships through a collection donated by Mr. and Mrs. Albert L. Partridge.

Connecticut Tall Clock by Silas Hoadley.
Wooden movement with ivory bushings.

Queen Anne Doll, 18th Century, Wood with Crewel Embroidered Dress

English Lady, 18th Century, Wood, Glass Eyes, Painted Features

"Aunt Peggy" — Mid 19th Century, Wood

"Grannie, won't you please make me another doll?"

—*Mrs. J. Watson Webb,*
Address at Colonial Williamsburg, *1958*

Over the centuries, how many grandmothers have heard such words as these? They hide the ageless wish of little girls all over the world, for no country is bereft of some kind of doll. It is a cherished companion of childhood and, often, even of a whole lifetime. Dolls were the lifelong interest of Mrs. Webb who received her earliest dolls from her maternal Grandmother, Matilda Waldron Elder.

Dolls are not always playthings. Some have religious significances such as the Indian dolls, and others were intended to attract customers as were the French fashion dolls. Few substances have been left untried in their manufacture — leather, wood, porcelain, rags, wax, papier mâché, and so on. Even a dried apple could be molded into a face whose wrinkles wouldn't matter to the feminine instincts of its owner.

After a labyrinthine amble through the first floor of the Variety Unit, the visitor suddenly finds himself upstairs, where the beckoning eyes of a thousand dolls search for "mama." Displayed according to the type of material from which they are made, they span the entire history of America, as well as depict the modes of its costume.

"Drolosse" — Late 19th Century, Parisian French Fashion Doll

"Ophelia" — Late 18th Century, Wax Head and Wooden Body

Hingham Massachusetts Lady, Early 19th Century, Stuffed Homespun

Fisherman, Late 19th Century, Stuffed Kid, Composition Head, Wooden Hands

English Doll, Mid 18th Century, Wood with Horsehair Wig

19

Rarity . . . . is always a quality to reckon with in putting together a collection. It is the quest for the seemingly unreachable that enlivens the hunt and spurs the true collector to seek those things of which dreams are made. Here, grouped around a diorama of the early American kitchen, are four pieces rightly called "rare."

A frieze on this porcelain Punch Bowl depicts "The Hongs at Canton," the "factories" or trading headquarters of the foreigners at Canton, China, their respective flags flying in the courtyards. Chinese Export Porcelain is also called Oriental Lowestoft. The English potters at Lowestoft used similar patterns and even signed their own name to Chinese pieces.

Three patterns of pressed glass, made by Gillender and Sons of Philadelphia, became especially popular in the late nineteenth century: Classic, Lion and Westward-Ho. Partly clear and partially acid frosted, this scalloped edge plate of the Classic pattern depicts a mounted warrior attacking a lion. The designer's name, P. J. Jacobus, is inscribed on the stone at the lower right.

A "Susan's Tooth" — one of nine known sperm whale teeth carved in 1829 by Frederick Myrick, while sailing "The Ship Susan of Nantucket," a whaler working off Japan. Carving ivory with jackknife or pickwick relieved the monotony of sea life between catches. Scrimshaw folk art produced many useful items as well as trinkets.

This molded glass dish has a diameter of twenty-four inches, and pieces of glass that size are extremely rare. McKee and Brothers, a glass house in Pittsburgh, Pennsylvania, is suggested as the manufacturer. Dated about 1865, few companies were equipped to make glass items of such proportions.

Oriental porcelain has always found acceptance in Europe and America, but the rising tea trade of the eighteenth century flooded both continents with hard paste porcelains which served as a profitable ballast in the merchantmen and later in the clipper ships. The market for this inexpensive china, often painted to order with armorial bearings and crests, was so brisk that foreign importers kept agents at "factories" in Canton.

This collection of Chinese Export Porcelain is a gift to Shelburne Museum of Mr. George G. Frelinghuysen.

THE TOY SHOP

A small, quaint brick addition on the west end of the Variety Unit houses the museum toys. It is a children's world which more often finds greater appreciation among the elders who wistfully gaze at playthings made to withstand usage, simple in their concept, and able to provide many hours of happy entertainment.

Toys were not always meant to entertain. To reassemble this educational knock-down doll required a great deal of manual dexterity. If play was considered sinful, the bible could be fun. How many Sundays saw processions of animals wending their way across the parlor floor into the ark, hardly reminding the child that "every living substance was destroyed which was upon the face of the earth."

Toys reduce a real world to a child's eye. Often they remove the prejudices of adults and whitewash the ills of society; sometimes toys could foster them.

Childhood is an age of innocence, as the portrait of a *Child Holding Toy Spaniel* reflects. It is a time of intense living, and that is no small accomplishment.

Unconcerned about reality, a child enjoys a little world. He pushes his trains from room to room, hissing and whistling all the way, or unloads his homemade steamboat at a miniature wharf perhaps made by his father.

THE VERGENNES SCHOOLHOUSE

Development of an educational system in the colonies was rapid. New England children were required to learn their fear of God by reading, and higher education was aimed at filling pulpits. At first, any vacant room or empty outbuilding served for a classroom, since proper facilities never kept pace with the desire for learning. Indeed, the "little red schoolhouse" perpetrated by Artemus Ward's novel was not common until after the Civil War.

Where separate buildings were set aside for education, religious conviction influenced the architecture of the school building in many instances. In New England, the schoolhouse was oftentimes a meeting house in miniature. A schoolhouse, with all the straightforward lines of the New England meeting house, was built at Vergennes, Vermont, in 1830 by General Samuel Strong. The town rented the school for one kernel of Indian maize, paid annually. Should the town no longer use it for education, the property was to revert to his heirs.

Cast to the elements when modern methodology replaced the one room school, many eyes sorrowfully watched the little school deteriorate until the museum acquired the building and moved it in 1947. It was the first of many buildings to make the trip to Shelburne.

"What you are to be you are now becoming."

Made of "pink" brick of varying shades, a row of headers, or bricks on end, encircles the building every seventh row. The schoolhouse sports a belfry with a copper dome replacing the original tin one and an acorn finial which once served as a target for youthful sharp-shooters.

Securing the building was no easy task, as it entailed opening the General's estate, closed now for some one hundred years. But effort was rewarded. Visitors now cross a threshold once crossed by generations of Vergennes school children. They pause, perhaps, to examine the initials of many, carved beside the doorway.

The schoolroom refurbished and Mrs. J. Watson Webb enjoying the front seat. Acquisition of the schoolhouse fulfilled a forty year dream of Mr. and Mrs. Webb, and the museum saw a newer horizon.

THE HORSESHOE BARN

The first building constructed at the museum was this great barn, a maze of some 668 rafters, knee braces, carrying posts and cross timbers. A search for a suitable barn to house a carriage collection brought to light a large horseshoe-shaped barn near Georgia, Vermont, and it was decided to use this as a model, altering some of the features to improve its proportions and symmetry.

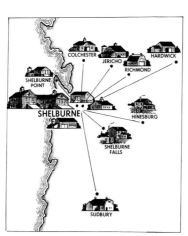

The project required an immense amount of material, and eventually, the museum crew under the skillful direction of Robert R. Francis dismantled eleven old barns and two grist mills to obtain the necessary beams. From these same barns came some of the slate for the roof and almost all of the seventeen thousand feet of boarding which covers the framework. New clapboards for the exterior were specially cut to reproduce the markings of an up and down saw. Completed, and crowned with three exquisitely proportioned cupolas, this barn is an apotheosis of joinery, for its framework is mortised and pegged together throughout.

The era of "the horse and buggy," romanticized in Edward Lamson Henry's *Carriage Ride on a Country Lane,* was dominated at its peak by rigid rules of etiquette and fashion. Although the Buggy was king, and a prized possession when families could afford one, among the affluent every occasion demanded its own particular carriage, properly horsed, with correct harness and with liveried servants. Lack of conformity raised the eyebrows of one's peers and brought on the unwillingness of certain carriage makers to welcome his business.

Dr. William Seward Webb, who thoroughly enjoyed a Buggy and a pair of fast steppers, built a Coach House, at his country estate in Shelburne, to house the horses and the carriages his social position required. Here, no detail was overlooked in caring for vehicles which were so highly polished that parts of them were reflected in the varnished foot-boards.

Driving four was the highest accomplishment of the "gentleman coachman." He took fresh pride in turning out a Road Coach or Park Drag horsed by a matched team and tooling it around the park — the roof seats filled with happy friends. Being elected to membership in the New York Coaching Club was the accolade earnestly sought for such ability and this honor came to Dr. Webb in 1887.

Dr. Webb on the box seat of the Road Coach "Pioneer" about to embark on a four-day trip to Shelburne Farms — longest annual drive of the New York Coaching Club.

The Coach House at The Farms contained many fine carriages, and after the death of Dr. Webb in 1926, they languished there, relics of another age, wistfully set aside to endure the quiet senility of neglect. When another use was found for the Coach House, a proposal to dispose of the vehicles was countered by Mr. and Mrs. J. Watson Webb, who offered to create a home for them where the public might enjoy seeing them. So in 1947, Shelburne Museum was born, and the construction of the Horseshoe Barn was started.

Of the twenty carriages which came to the museum, an exquisite Berlin and an equally beautiful Caleche are superb examples of the coachmaker's art. Both were built in 1890 by the Parisian firm of Million and Guiet.

The open Caleche is suitable for only the most formal calling or park work; it is a state class vehicle. The Berlin, one of the oldest of carriage types, was used on great festive occasions. Its interior trimming is unequalled.

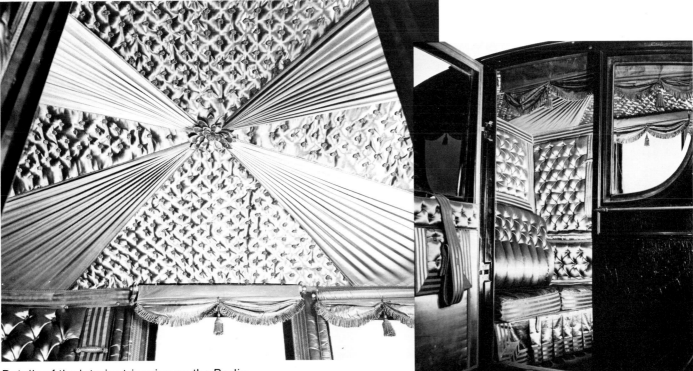

Details of the interior trimming on the Berlin.

Gifts of other carriages made the vehicle collection almost complete. James Hazen Hyde's famous Road Coach "Liberty," a gift of Mr. J. Ford Johnson, brought one of the most historic coaches in America to the museum. Mr. Hyde drove it in Switzerland to the top of St. Bernard's pass and later, with Mr. Alfred Gwynne Vanderbilt, set a record run in the "Liberty" of 19 hours, 35 minutes, New York to Philadelphia and return.

"Going-to-Cover" Cart, gift of Mrs. Richard V. N. Gambrill.

Display of coaching harness and accessories, along with several of some hundred or more trophies won by Mr. J. Watson Webb on the polo field.

The rare Curricle, proper two-wheeled carriage for a pair of horses. The center pole is suspended from a bar across the backs of the horses.

Thanksgiving Day was the traditional time to switch from Buggy to sleigh. In fact, many people postponed business trips until winter when travel over snow was easier and quicker. Fancy driving cutters and country sleighs, such as these, vied for an open stretch of road, where tinkling sleigh bells, or crotals, merrily urged on the horses. Stage sleighs, like this one which ran for over one hundred years between Worcester and Lowell, Massachusetts, carried travelers bundled in fur robes — their feet warmed by embers in the foot warmers. The winter snows settled a new beauty upon an autumn's demise. Regrettably, the horseless carriage did not settle as much on its own new era.

THE SHAKER SHED

Farm buildings are basically similar and differ because one locale, or even one individual, chooses to accentuate one or another of their structural details. Growth of business often requires additions, and a farmer enlarges his barn or extends his shed to accommodate his needs. A farm building becomes, as it were, a chronicle in wood, of success on the land and of fruitful labor.

The Shaker community at East Canterbury, New Hampshire, started such a "chronicle" in 1834. They built a horse stand to shelter horses and carriages. Needing storage space for the brooms they were making and marketing, the Shakers added, in 1850, a story and a half above it. Later, in 1853, they added a shed at the rear for farm machinery. The final building was 86 feet long, some 40 feet wide, and two and one half stories high.

The building was plain but sturdy, for the Shakers spurned ornamentation as superfluous. Nonetheless, the facade boasts five granite columns which bestow an enrichment its former owners would not have considered worldly. These five pillars, in a sense, signify the very durability of the structure and the inner strength of its builders. Renovated and restored, it houses a multitude of tools and household implements built around a large woodworking tool collection presented to the museum by Frank H. Wildung. He also created the displays in this Shaker Shed.

"Hands to work and heart to God."

Religious conviction brought new colonists to the Americas and their beliefs determined the way of life in those settlements for which they were responsible. The Shakers, one of the many religious sects to take root in America, not only perfected a way of life for themselves but also exerted a wide influence on the manner of life and the habits of their fellow Americans.

Theirs was a particular ingenuity for arranging a life style that was simple, plain and unadorned. To achieve this, they invented a wide variety of items appropriate for so tidy a people. These they shared with their neighbors, for they were just as industrious in supporting themselves as in saving their souls. They long dominated the garden seed market and their herb medicines were much in demand.

Their gaunt but nobly proportioned buildings have survived. Even more prized is their furniture. With pure lines, a natural grace and symmetry, spare and exceedingly strong, Shaker furniture is the legacy of their belief. Whether it carries the trademark or not, it shall remain indicative of a life style guided by principle.

"The house is very handsome and perfectly furnished ..." *Marquis de Chastellux*

A true craftsman consistently produces wares which have an inherent beauty about them. It is nearly always instantaneously apparent that he has imbued his work with quality. Between that craftsman and his product stands the tool with which he achieves his result. Technology may have brought sophistication to the tools of the various trades, but additions to the basic components of a tool chest have been few. Most tools retain a simple design that belies their potential in the hands of a master craftsman. But, by and large, to understand the craftsman and his craft, one must comprehend the tool; perhaps, even find in it a beauty all its own.

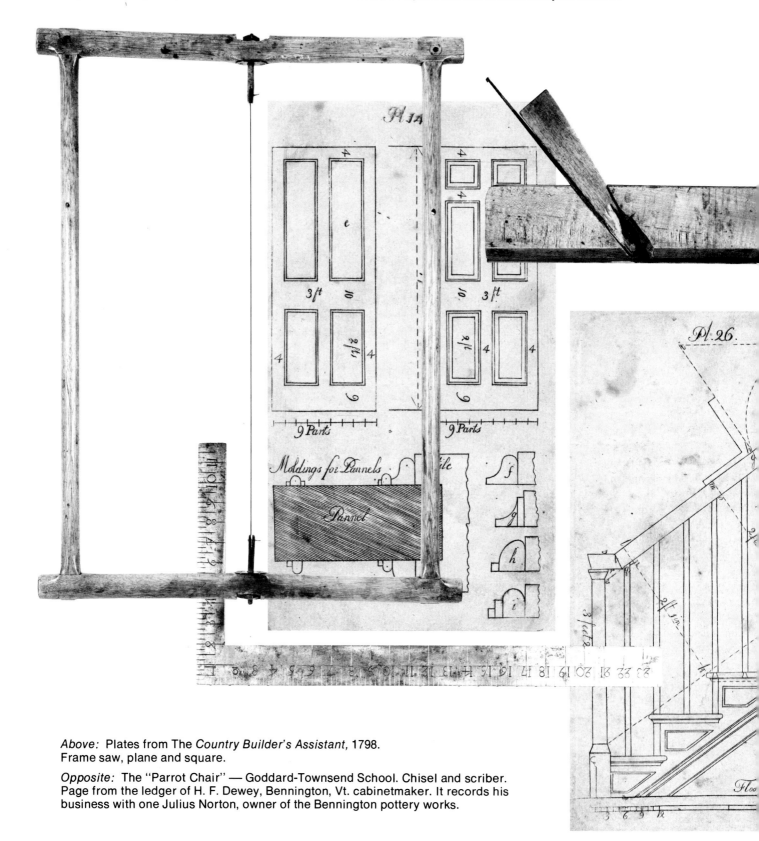

Above: Plates from The *Country Builder's Assistant,* 1798.
Frame saw, plane and square.

Opposite: The "Parrot Chair" — Goddard-Townsend School. Chisel and scriber.
Page from the ledger of H. F. Dewey, Bennington, Vt. cabinetmaker. It records his business with one Julius Norton, owner of the Bennington pottery works.

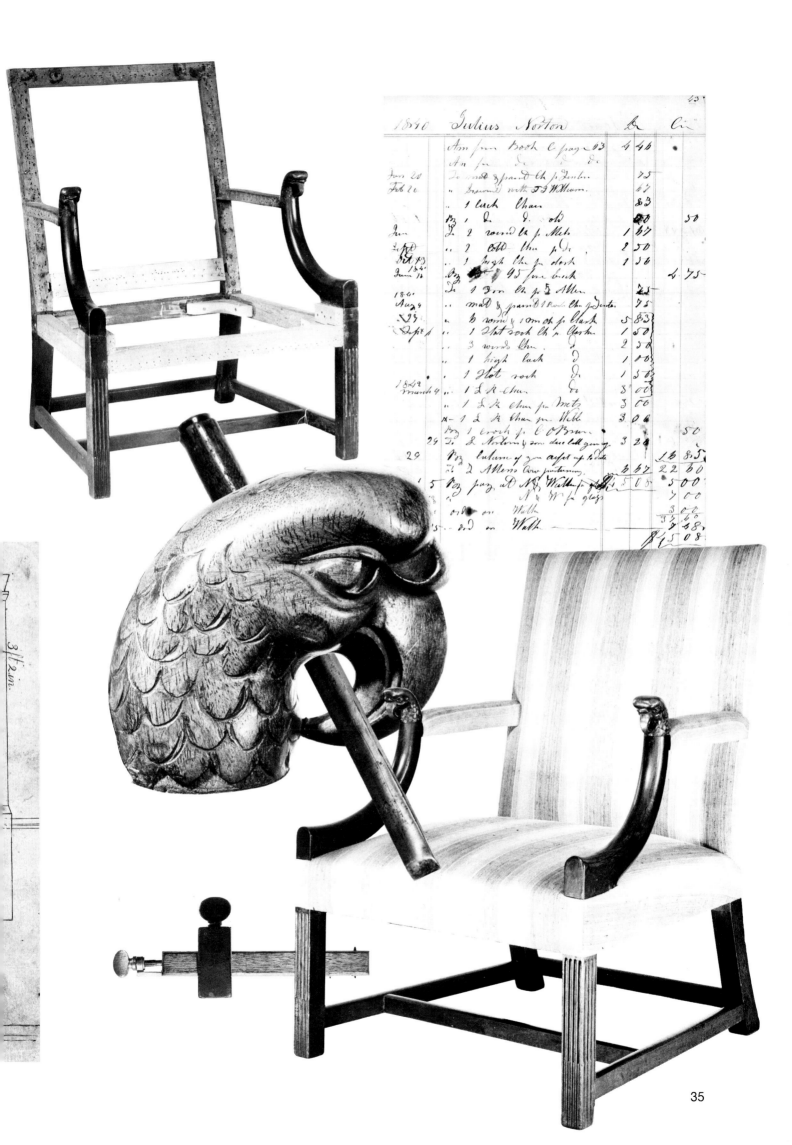

It is not easy to harness or to saddle a horse properly. Poorly fitted or poorly made, harness can quickly offend the rigid rules of equine fashion and may even injure or cripple the animal. A horse works easily and comfortably in quality harness which is well-chosen and well-cared for.

One of two trade shops set up in the Shaker Shed, The Harnessmaker and Saddler's Shop is replete with every item required for his work. A cabinet on the wall holds rows of punches, pliers and other assorted tools, and on the bench nearby lies the crescent-shaped leather knife peculiar to the craft. The drawers are full of buckles, and bits and pieces of leather hang about the room.

Harness Advertisement from *Moseman's Illustrated Guide,* 1890

BLACKSMITH AND WHEELWRIGHT SHOP

Nobody knows exactly when a blacksmith first opened the doors of this shop for business. The original single workroom of handmade brick was built sometime around 1800. Business evidently flourished there, necessitating a wooden frame addition at the rear. Here a wheelwright made light carriages, sleighs and wagons and did repair work. Up front, a smithy heated iron in his forge and hammered out his wares on the anvil. Over the years, a succession of blacksmiths occupied the building — John Dubuc, Joe White, and a Mr. Guilette among them. By 1935, it stood empty, as the automobile had muscled the horse and buggy aside and mass-produced ironwork from large foundries reduced the market for the blacksmith's handiwork. The building was rapidly becoming a derelict when it was acquired by the museum in 1956. The crumbling walls were shored up by a newly poured concrete foundation and the entire structure moved in two sections to the grounds. Restored and refitted, a smithy's "music" occasionally reverberates within when the old forge is fired up and the anvil is once more put to good use.

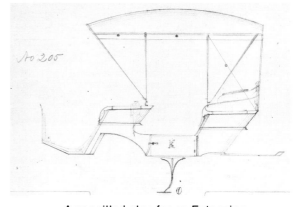

A pencilled plan for an Extension Top Park Phaeton by Hobbs Bros., Nineveh, N.Y. The carriage was built around 1875 for G. A. Kent of Binghamton, N.Y.

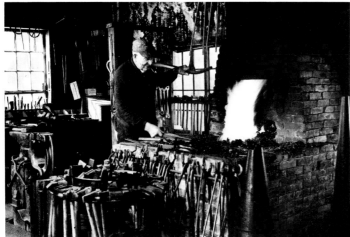

There was a great demand for blacksmiths, and as a matter of fact, they headed the list of tradesmen solicited by the Virginia Company for its settlement at Jamestown. By definition, a blacksmith's work was limited to fashioning pieces of handwork from iron, but they gradually assumed a number of related tasks. Since they made horseshoes, it was only natural for them to, also, set them to the horses' hooves. Thus, they became farriers as well.

Iron Farrier's Sign, 19th Century

Blacksmith's Weathervane,
Iron and Zinc, Late 19th Century

Out of hundreds of small carriage shops,
like this, rolled a multitude of light, easy-to-
make vehicles and wagons. Miscellaneous
parts were stock-piled from jobbers and assembled into a wide assortment of small
carriages. However, a neighborhood wheelwright spent most of his time mending and
patching local conveyances which just
needed upkeep. He replaced spokes, set
new tires, made new shafts, reupholstered
seats, or built new tops. Some wheelwrights
marketed a specialty vehicle peculiarly their
own.

Einars J. Mengis

THE COLCHESTER REEF LIGHTHOUSE

The casual appearance and apparent nonchalant attitude of these five "tourists" on the lighthouse platform altogether belies the nature of the place. Three miles off Allen Point, southernmost tip of Grande Isle, and just under one mile off Colchester Point, lies one of the most treacherous reefs in Lake Champlain. Here in 1871 the Lighthouse Service erected a frame structure strong enough to withstand the sudden gales of spring and fall and the pressure of the winter ice floes. For 62 years, eleven different keepers kept the light going until the lighthouse was decommissioned in 1933. Electricity had, at last, reached Colchester Reef.

"Jack Tar" — Ship Chandler's Sign, c. 1860-1870

Lake Champlain had been the silent sentinel, as two great nations struggled for control of the continent. French and English ships replaced Indian canoes, as both realized that this north-south water highway was the key to dominance. In 1776, Benedict Arnold took on King George's navy behind Valcour Island across the lake. During the War of 1812, Lt. Thomas Macdonough defeated the British fleet in Plattsburgh Bay off Cumberland Head. Too late for all of this, the lighthouse did play a vital role when the steamship was master of the "inland sea."

As recognition of Lake Champlain's historical importance gained wider appreciation, relics and artifacts from her waters became great prizes. Few, however, could see the day when technology would change the pattern of life on the lake. Already one last sidewheeler was fighting for life when, in 1952, the Coast Guard auctioned off the Colchester Reef Lighthouse. The museum purchased the building from the only bidder, and a courageous crew of five men moved it off the shoals. Now it is a gallery of marine art and history.

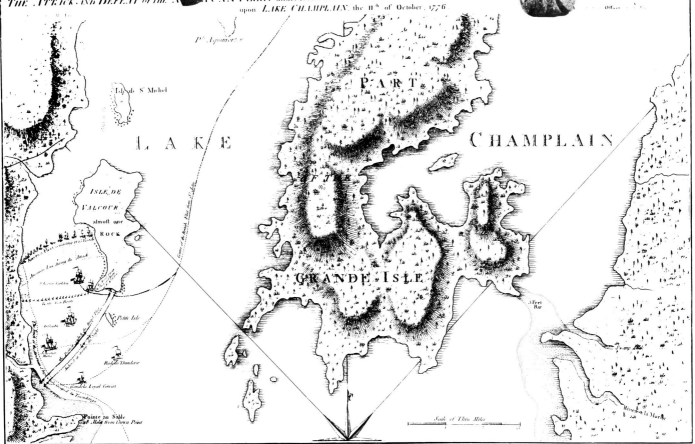

Figurehead, New England, c. 1830-1840

"And All I Ask is a Tall Ship..." *John Masefield*

U.S. Ship "Pennsylvania"
Lithograph by L. P. Clover

Steam Ship "Savannah"
Lithograph by G. Hayward

The Emily Reed
by C. W. Goucher, c. 1881

Naval Battle
Anonymous

The Ship "Ohio"
by Thomas Birch, 1829

Clipper Ship "Flying Cloud"
Lithograph by N. Currier

The "Portugese Sailor" Tavern Sign, Maine, Late 19th Century

"... there floated into my inmost soul, endless processions of the whale ..."

Herman Melville, Moby Dick

For profit and pleasure men have hunted even the largest denizens of the earth regardless of the danger. Few of them, however, have written an entire chapter in history as did the whalers. Sharp-eyed salts from New England towns, such as New Bedford or Sag Harbor, spent sometimes three years at sea in order to bring back a shipload of whale oil, spermaceti and the rare ambergris. The excitement of the chase and the thrill of the great Nantucket sleigh ride has been well portrayed by lithographers. Many of their prints, together with pieces of scrimshaw and other mementoes have found a way to the whaling gallery at the Colchester Reef Lighthouse.

"Hugest of living creatures, in the deep
Stretched like a promontory sleeps or swims,
and seems a moving land; and at his gills
Draws in, and at his breath spouts out a sea."

John Milton, Paradise Lost

44

THE DUTTON HOUSE

In 1949, museum officials were invited to Cavendish, Vermont, to view an ancient salt box which had recently been donated to the Vermont Historical Society. This was the house of Salmon Dutton, who came to Vermont in 1781, from Ashby, Massachusetts. The rambling house, with its dark red clapboards and shingled roof, was built a year later in 1782. For over a century, the house had remained a home for Dutton's descendents, and then about 1900 finally fell vacant although it was maintained by a respectful family. By the time the house came into the hands of the Vermont Historical Society, it had been unoccupied for 50 years. The Society, having no means for preserving early buildings, offered the house to Shelburne Museum.

The Dutton House, having stood empty so long, fortunately escaped the renovations which have wrought such damage to many of America's historic buildings. As found in 1949, it was almost unaltered from its original appearance. Meticulous disassembly and reconstruction was completed in early 1951, after which relatively little restorative work was needed.

In furnishing the house, the concept of "period rooms" was rejected. Instead, pieces of furniture have been grouped together in the more realistic manner of a family accumulation gathered by successive generations of thrifty New Englanders.

It may well have been the personal fancies of Salmon Dutton, himself, that dictated the design of his house at Cavendish. Perhaps it was the uncertainty of Vermont's quasi-frontier environment and unsettled political situation that caused Dutton to seek security in the choice of a familiar design that had been in use for 100 years. We can also picture Dutton, the practical farmer, pounding his fist on the table to emphasize his determination to add a Beverly jog and an ell, each where they would do the most good. In practice, the jog on the left of the house would provide room for a buttery adjacent to the kitchen, while the ell, not quite perpendicular to the rear, would include an extra room, sheds and additional attic space.

Yet Dutton, as a man of property and community position, certainly wished his house to reflect his status. For years, English architects had been finding inspiration in the order and symmetry of Greek and Roman examples, and for some time, such ideas had been gaining currency in America. Would a classical style porch, window moldings, and cornice dentil work be incongruous with an asymmetrical country salt box? Dutton thought not! To his plan conceived of Yankee conservation and utility, he added this measure of Georgian respectability, and as we look at the house today, we cannot but agree with his choices.

THE PRENTIS HOUSE

Built in 1733 by the Dickenson family of Hadley, Massachusetts, this house is the oldest building at the museum and is preserved in its original, unaltered design. A true saltbox type, it was exquisitely furnished with pieces germane to its age by Katherine Prentis Murphy for whom it was named.

The *Dining Room* contains a collection of English delft, set out on an oak gate-leg table, as well as a Pilgram oak and pine Court Cupboard. Bannister-back chairs are set about the room and from a rack close by gleam pieces of polished pewter.

The *Dining Room Chamber* features a lovely Queen Anne Highboy, with walnut veneer and herringbone inlay and a post bed with a rare set of crewel hangings and valance. Sleeping rooms on the second story were called chambers and were differentiated by using the name of the rooms beneath them.

The house recommended itself for preservation not only because of the original sheathing and floor boards, but also because of the unusual brickwork. The various flues converge on the second floor in a massive "beehive" which extends upward of eight feet before reverting to the conventional rectangular chimney.

The *Kitchen,* stripped of its wallpapers and grit, is complete with the latest in 17th century cookware. Pewter chargers decorate the mantleboard, and burl bowls stand ready on the table and the New England Chest. By the fireside stands a bannister-back armchair with high arms and turned front posts with mushroom finials.

THE VERMONT HOUSE

Asa Slocum came to East Shelburne, Vermont, in 1790. His second home was a frame building with a clapboard exterior which he built around his log cabin. When the exterior was complete, he dismantled the cabin and carried it out the front door.

With a front entrance hall and fireplace rather than the customary staircase, the building was of museum caliber. Weathered stone from the Shelburne Gristmill was substituted for the deteriorated clapboarding which could not be saved.

Envisioned as a retired sea captain's home, the *Dining Room* boasts Chippendale side chairs with flame stitch upholstery and a mahogany Queen Anne Table. The antique French wallpapers are unique. The appointments are Waterford and Whieldon.

Courtesy of Charles Tuttle Company

Courtesy ANTIQUES MAGAZINE

Photo by C. Robert Callahan

Activities in the *Kitchen* centered around this massive brick fireplace and bake oven. An octagonal hutch table dominates the area, and nearby is a pine settle of unusually wide boards. On the wall above it, a clock jack is wound, ready to turn the roast.

At one end of the Kitchen, where one might expect to find a pantry, he is pleasantly surprised by this cozy nook. A two drawer, oak and pine, Hadley chest stands against the wall, and there is a writing-arm Windsor in the corner. Delft tile pictures hang on the wall, and pieces of slip ware sit upon the table. A delft rooster seems about to crow from the windowsill.

Photo by C. Robert Callahan

Furnished with examples of America's finest furniture, the *Parlor* reflects a cosmopolitan taste and affluence. Here Queen Anne pieces predominate — a gaming table and its chairs, nestled in the corner, needs only some jovial players; and a looking glass hung above the cherry lowboy, reflects a lacquered highboy on the opposite wall. The large cherry secretary on-frame may well be the work of the Connecticut craftsman, Benjamin Burham. The closed bonnet top with candy twist finials soars above the arched and panelled doors. Its frame stands on cabriole legs with Dutch feet.

Sitting before the fireplace, arranged for tea, are three of the most notable pieces of furniture at Shelburne. The octagonal, dish top Queen Anne tea table, with a small collar carved below each knee, has very delicately shaped legs which end in a paw and pad foot. In spite of an unorthodox design, it has all the characteristics of a Newport piece. Drawn up on its right is an exquisite Queen Anne arm chair with scrolled and knuckled arms and shell carved knees. The gift of Mr. George Frelinghuysen, it is attributed to the Philadelphia cabinetmaker William Savery. Across the table is a chair justifiably termed unique. Ascribed to the Goddard-Townsend School of Newport, R.I., the "Parrot Chair" carries the transitional features of both the Chippendale and Hepplewhite periods. Connecticut "cathedral" panelling completes a truly remarkable setting.

Photo by C. Robert Callahan

The Vermont House *Parlor*

53

The Dutton House *Kitchen*

This compact little cottage from Columbus, N.Y., dates from about the year 1790. Stenciling as a form of interior decoration was popular in the early 19th century and served as a less expensive counterpart to imported wallpapers. The men who stenciled such wall designs were generally itinerant artists, and their distinctive styles, traced from house to house, mark their travels through New England, across New York and west as far as Indiana. Some of the design elements, shown here, suggest the work of Moses Eaton, the noted stenciler from New Hampshire.

The *Kitchen* is generally the center of family activity and appropriately enough; it is the most spacious room in the Stencil House.

The wide pine boards which form the wall sheathing in the *Dining Room* give a good indication of the size of the timber available to our ancestors. Arrangement of the wall panelling varies, with interior partitions and fireplace walls finished in vertical boards while the interiors of the outside walls are done in horizontal boards.

This cozy bed chamber under the eaves with its fireplace and wing chair might well cause us to reconsider the worth of some of our modern "improvements."

Courtesy of ANTIQUES MAGAZINE

The "Cape Cod" styling of the Stencil House is perhaps the most persistent form in American architecture. Its direct ancestor was the thatch roofed, white washed cottage of Elizabethan England with walls made of clay and lime mixture. New England's dry spells made the thatch roof dangerously inflammable, and its driving storms simply eroded such walls away. Very early colonists adopted shingles and clapboards to keep out the weather and the resulting house style has remained popular right up to the present.

THE STAGECOACH INN

The tavern stand from Charlotte, Vermont, dates from the unsettled years following the Revolution when Vermont was an independent Republic. Its builder, Hezakiah Barnes, seems to have been one of those dynamic frontier individuals who appear in the annals of every frontier locality. His activities included town moderator, selectman, surveyor of highways, school clerk, member of the meeting house committee, Captain in the militia and town representative in the legislature.

In addition to his civic activities, he found time to prosper as a storekeeper and establish himself as an innkeeper on the stage route between Canada and Southern New England. His spacious Inn with its 10 fireplaces must have been an island of warmth and congeniality for many hungry travelers.

Outside the Inn stands the old-time stagecoach passenger signal. The ball lowered, it signaled the driver to stop and take on passengers. The raised position, or "highball," indicated that no stop was necessary.

Copper Eagle—Late 19th Century, N.Y.C.

It is fitting that the Stagecoach Inn, whose years coincide so closely with those of our national period, should house a collection of Americana including so many examples of our national emblem—the eagle. The degree of popularity, enjoyed by the eagle as a decorative device, testifies to the patriotic fervor in the new nation. Professional artists and country craftsmen alike tried their hands at capturing its likeness. The birds appeared, made of every conceivable material, in an astounding variety of poses, for an infinite number of perches, positions, and purposes. Significantly, the eagles took on all the diversity of the heterogeneous nation they had come to represent.

Wooden Eagle—19th Century, Massachuse[t]

Wooden Eagle—19th Century, N.Y.C.

Iron and Tin Eagle—
19th Century, Maine

Wooden Eagle by Wilhelm Schimmel,
c. 1875, Pennsylvania

Cigar Store Figure, Probably by Charles or Samuel A. Robb, c.1900

The Stagecoach Inn's collection of American wood sculpture traces the progress of the carver's art over more than a century of development. Earliest are the figureheads and associated ship's decorations which long represented the mainstay of the carver's business. During the mid 19th century, disruptions within the shipping industry caused carvers to look for other markets. Thousands of urban tobacco stores, tea shops and newsstands were ready customers and so followed decades of cigar store Indians and other shop front characters. Finally, the colorful world of the circus with its ornately carved wagons kept the carvers busy into the early 20th century.

"Columbia" — Ship's Figurehead, Anonymous, Mid 19th Century

"Thomas Dartmouth Rice as Jim Crow" — Shop Figure, Attributed to Charles J. Dodge, c.1840

Circus Wagon Figure, by Samuel A. Robb, c.1886

"George Washington" — Ship's Figurehead, Anonymous, Early or Mid 19th Century

Weather Creatures of the Stagecoach Inn

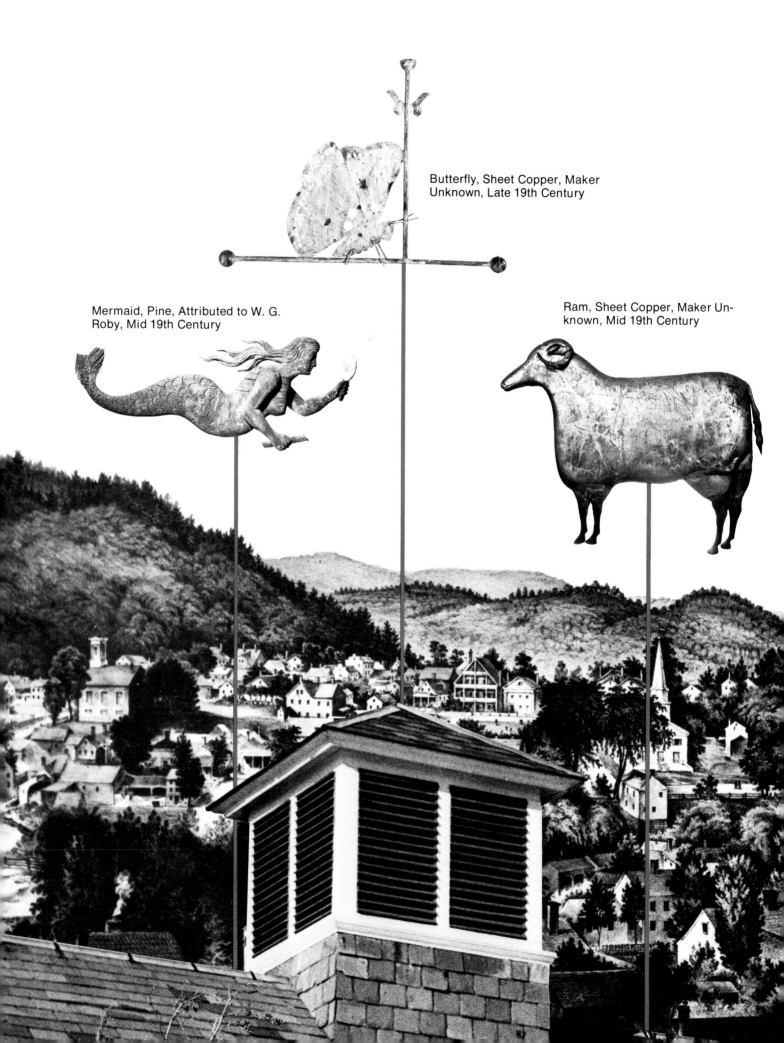

Butterfly, Sheet Copper, Maker Unknown, Late 19th Century

Mermaid, Pine, Attributed to W. G. Roby, Mid 19th Century

Ram, Sheet Copper, Maker Unknown, Mid 19th Century

"Liberty" — Sheet Copper, Cushing Company, Waltham, Mass., c.1860-85

"Bareback Rider" — Sheet Copper, Maker Unknown, Late 19th Century

"Massasoit" — Sheet Copper, Harris Company, Boston, Mass., Last Quarter 19th Century

"The Lion Killer" — Sheet Iron, Maker Unknown, Late 19th Century

THE STONE COTTAGE

Found in 1947 as a bare stone shell, the little cottage from South Burlington seemed almost beyond hope of restoration. Its masonry, however, showed rare quality, and the building was recognized as too valuable an example to leave to the elements. After the building was purchased, its limestone walls were covered to keep out the weather until the museum's busy schedule could find time for the move. Then in 1949, the stones were individually numbered and the building was removed piece by piece to the museum grounds.

Fate smiled on the Stone Cottage when a newspaper article about the removal reached an elderly Burlington resident, a direct descendant of the original owner of the building. Her recollections of the interior, as it had looked 80 years before, enabled the otherwise impossible duplication of the original floor plan. She still remembered much about the dairy laborer and his family who had once lived in the house and even was able to provide the original wrought iron door latch which she had removed years before as the building had begun to slip into ruins. Restoration was completed with old beams and materials from several local barns, homes and derelict buildings.

The Stone Cottage, its warm spirit revived, stands silent witness to the fact that across our country many treasures lie at the very gates of the junkyard or sit perilously close to destruction. The cottage represents a small victory in the continuing struggle to preserve the many fine examples of our cultural heritage for our own enrichment and for the enjoyment of future generations of Americans.

CASTLETON JAIL

How does one go about moving a 50 ton stone building 64 miles? This was the very question that faced the Museum in 1953 when it bought Castleton Jail. The slate and brick construction of the 1890 structure presented a picture of incredible weight and solidity, yet the jail's compactness (16' x 20') made it possible to move its four walls without dismantling them. Removing the floor, roof, interior fittings, and gables lightened it enough to be jacked into the air, fitted with wheels, and slowly pulled to Shelburne.

Tearing down the jail's gables offered no problem in itself, but looking ahead, it became clear that measures should be taken to insure accurate rebuilding. To make this possible the gables were framed in wood, crisscrossed with a grid of string, numbered, and photographed. This system enabled perfect registration of every stone for reconstruction at the Museum.

When Henry David Thoreau described his overnight jail cell at Concord, Massachusetts, he mentioned its two windows, whitewashed walls and called it the "neatest apartment in the town." Had he been incarcerated at Castleton, Vermont, his remarks would certainly have been more harsh. As it sits at Shelburne Museum, the jail's picturesque slate walls hide a dark cold interior of stone and iron where the visitor is happy to make his visit a brief one.

THE TUCKAWAY GENERAL STORE
AND APOTHECARY SHOP

A handsome Greek revival example from nearby Shelburne Center, this building for years served as the village post office. In 1952 it traveled ¼ mile over a specially laid railroad track to be pressed into service as the Museum's General Store. Typically a multiple use building, the store includes a barber shop, post office, tap room, Doctors and Dentists offices and an Apothecary Shop. With such a collection of functions it is easy to see how the general store was second only to the meeting house as a community gathering place.

Occupying a central position inside the General Store is the iron stove which was a favored gathering place for the exchange of news during the cold months of the year. Today's visitor finds a staggering array of goods on shelves, on racks, or hanging at every available space just as they were displayed in countless country stores a century ago. Even present are the pungent aromas of aging cheese, dried fish, wintergreen and the like making the very air in the store authentic of the period.

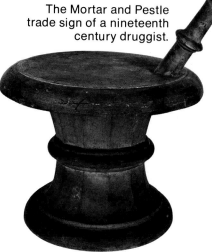

The Mortar and Pestle trade sign of a nineteenth century druggist.

Grant Heilman

If the mortar and pestle was first in importance to the apothecary's business, then certainly the bottle was second. In bottles arrived unusual herbs, barks and medicinal components from distant lands. In bottles his preparations were stored, and later sold to the customer. In his windows they even served as decoration and a secondary symbol of his trade. And today, these containers, so commonplace a century ago, are sought by collectors for their color, their shapes and their amusing claims.

When viewed in light of twentieth century pharmaceutical practice, the lost life style of the old-time apothecary seems a bizarre existence. Before the days of drug companies and wholesale suppliers these men spent endless hours gathering herbs, drying and grinding them and extracting their medicinal components by means of percolators such as the one pictured.

Following the Civil War, the industrial boom that swept the country had its medicinal counterpart in large scale commercialization of drugs. As the twentieth century approached, much of the apothecary's equipment fell into disuse while his shelves filled with bottles claiming to cure every conceivable ailment. The Shelburne Museum apothecary exhibit documents the progress of medical treatment from the days of herbal decoctions through the maze of the "patent," or proprietary, medicine period into the present century. On the shelves of this shop one may find everything from obvious frauds to time-tested remedies still on the market today.

THE DORSET HOUSE

As the Shelburne Museum began to take form in the late 1940's, no one could foresee the directions that expansion would take. Originally, all of the folk art, including the nucleus of the decoy collection, was displayed together in the Stagecoach Inn. With the addition of the decoy collection of Joel Barber, the noted writer and collector, it became apparent that the decoys needed a building of their own. In 1953, the museum located and moved from East Dorset, Vermont, a building ideally suited for display of these waterfowl carvings.

The house with its Greek revival lines, its elaborate cornices and columns, was, in spite of many years of neglect, a house worth saving. It had been built about 1840 and over much of its history had been a two-family dwelling. Inside, like most 19th century houses, the walls were simple and unpanelled, finished in plaster — a straightforward interior that allowed considerable flexibility for museum display.

In the several years following the reconstruction of the Dorset House, the numbers of examples on display grew at what seemed almost a geometric rate. During this period, the museum acquired a number of fine collections not only of working decoys but also including miniatures and display pieces. Paintings and hunting paraphernalia complete this picture of the old waterfowling days.

Since the Indians first contrived duck decoys in prehistoric times, their making has remained almost entirely an American craft and art form. Their construction of wood, solid and hollow, or of canvas-covered slats, of cork, of cardboard, or of metal, in dozens of species, covers a wide range of sophistication. Over the last two centuries, carvers have also found time to produce examples of shore birds which were lured and hunted in the same fashion as were ducks and geese. Dubbed with exotic names like curlew, knot, snipe, plover and dowicher, they strike a variety of standing poses producing a deceptive feeling of darting motion.

Confidence decoys, representing such non-game species as gulls, terns or even herons, like this one, were set among a duck hunter's stool to allay the fears of an approaching flock.

The Stuart M. Crocker Collection with its carvings by A. Elmer Crowell represents the most refined stage of the decoy maker's art. For these are delicate display pieces destined never to see the marshes or feel the bite of autumn's raw winds.

HAT & FRAGRANCE

The 19th Century failed to fully recognize the potential of its women and wastefully pressed them into an often dreary domestic mold. Restricted by the limited options of the times, women searched for acceptable outlets for their hidden creativity. In the needle, the thread, and the loom they found their mediums. The patience with which they accepted their roles was the very strength which made possible time consuming textile projects of tremendous complexity. Patience, skill and a sense of design, formed the combination which, in its attainments often gives the modern artist cause for admiration. In the rooms beyond the weathered boards of the old town barn hundreds of textile creations survive as the legacy of the 19th Century women.

Quilt Panel, Mariner's Compass, 1835

Throughout Colonial times and into the early years of our national period, the needlework projects of American women often started in the fields. Crewel embroidery, for instance, required the production of linen for background material. Flax, the plant used to make linen, had to be grown, harvested, soaked and then its non-fibrous material removed by working it through the jaws of a flax breaker such as the one pictured. Following this "breaking," the flax had to be combed on the teeth of a hetchel before spinning and weaving. And all this was just preparation for the intricate stitchery with wool yarns.

Awesome in its scale, the Hat & Fragrance Rug Room with its imposing collection of vertically hung handmade examples carries home the colossal proportions of American domestic textile endeavor. Huge gilded eagles and a furniture factory trade sign in the form of a massive rocking chair, nearly seven feet tall, combine with the rugs to present a scene that dwarfs the viewer.

Embroidered rug worked in wools on a background of black broadcloth.

77

Woven Worlds of Art

The 1820's witnessed the start of a momentous transition from home to factory weaving. Appearing in America at the same time and spanning this transition was the Jacquard loom which employed a roll of punched paper cards to govern the pattern of the weave. In the hands of a professional weaver, complex designs were possible and available to those who could afford the price of the craftsman's work. Floral, geometric, and pictorial designs with charming borders often including the name of the weaver are typical of the bed coverlets which these looms produced. Unfortunately, this stage in craftsmanship was temporary for about the time of the Civil War powered versions of the Jacquard loom replaced the weaver and his highly individualized product.

78

In a world of black and white . . .

In contrast to the colorful world of the quilts, coverlets and crewel, the lace and white-on-white embroidery displayed in the Hat and Fragrance stands apart for its subtlety. Used by ladies of the 1820's and 1830's to balance the staid dresses of the period, they have a refined elegance all their own. Such pieces have long been valued for their delicate beauty, each one the end result of months of work which made them the treasured luxuries of their day.

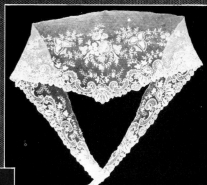

A bonnet, a cape and a black dress were "Sunday best" to be donned for a portrait sitting.

A masterpiece
white-on-whi
embroide
balanced b
asymmetric

THE MEETING HOUSE

. . . was built as a Methodist Church in 1840 at Charlotte, Vermont. After the parish ceased to function about 1900, the building was preserved as a library and theater. By 1950 when offered to Shelburne Museum, the Meeting House had suffered from years of decline, but its trim beauty, however soiled and disheveled, was still very much apparent.

Wrought Iron Church Finial
Maine, c. 1800

The Meeting House restoration presented several difficulties. Old photos revealed that, prior to 1909, the building had been surmounted by a wooden belfry. Fortunately, the museum was able to salvage a similar one from an old meeting house at Miltonboro, Vermont, along with pews and a pulpit to replace those of the Charlotte Meeting House which had long since disappeared. An interview with an elderly resident supplied information enabling duplication of the original interior layout.

The painted wall panels, executed by Duncan Munro of the museum staff, provide a finishing touch. The large rectangular sections are actually frescoes, water colors painted on wet plaster, which give a three dimensional effect so striking that visitors' hands invariably reach out to check the accuracy of their eyes.

Restored to its former dignity, the Charlotte Meeting House stands as a monument to the intense spirituality of the early New Englander and tells much about his faith. Its dim lighting and dearth of heating underscores his religious fortitude. Its simplicity bespeaks his Protestant view emphasizing the individual apart from ecclesiastical organization. Its beauty and position dramatize his total commitment to religion.

The Meeting House was a community focal point. It was the first public structure, the scene of social gatherings, the stage for political events, and above all the place for the public worship. Every important public undertaking began with a sermon and the success or failure of any enterprise was examined in a religious light. Even the weathercock on the belfry reminded that the cock's crowing a new dawn was, indeed, cause for awe, a reminder of Peter's denial of Christ and a warning of the passage of time and the nearness of the Almighty.

In a waning September moon, many a duck hunter would begin to watch the northern skies for soon to come down the great flyways were immense flocks of ducks and geese. Out of trunks, boxes, or boat bays came upwards of sometimes seventy or more decoys which he would set out in "rigs" to lure live birds from the air. Most of these decoys were carved of wood and hand painted. No species was neglected, and in a search for realism, no material was left untried. Several makers achieved a mastery in capturing the feathered likenesses, and their artistry was almost instinctive. Collectors will recognize works of Joel Barber, Lem Ward, "Shang" Wheeler and Harry Shourdes in this ice-ensnared stool of fakers.

Near perfect deception was the "confidence" decoy, headless ducks which appear to be feeding or sleepers like one of Captain Osgood's geese across the page. The ultimate trick was mixing a gull or crane among the decoys.

Color Courtesy of AMERICAN HERITAGE

Pêche de la Baleine. Aquatint by Martens. (From the Lighthouse Gallery)

The Hat & Fragrance

A visit to the Hat and Fragrance textile display is an exercise in perspective. One may view the boldness of the Star of Bethlehem Quilt from across the room or move closer to inspect the careful stitchery of the Mariner's compass at close range. The needlework is fine enough to compete with machine sewing, yet the projects are so complex that few women today would dare attempt them with modern equipment. Likewise, the coverlets hand woven a century ago, exhibit a richness and warmth not easily found today.

Winter in the Country: A Cold Morning. George Henry Durrie, 1862 (From the Webb Gallery of American Art)

Copper Horse —
c. 1850, Shelburne, Vt.

Copper Centaur —
19th Century, New Haven, Conn.

The Stagecoach Inn

Prior to the onslaught of industry, every man invested his work with the indelible signature of pride in his craftsmanship. No matter how utilitarian, "handmade" was a very conspicuous label, and even mundane items were shrouded in art. Consequently, carved figures, allegorical, mythological or otherwise perched on a ship's prow to catch the first froth of the ocean waves and battalions of "redskins" pushed tobacco along every sidewalk in town. Vast menageries were turned out in tinsmith's shops or on blacksmith's anvils to stare from every cupola in the county. Tavern signs swung from a host of inns, the work of an army of itinerant artists who painted for an ale or two.

Cigar Store Indian by Louis Jobin
Quebec, c. 1880

The S.S. Ticonderoga.

Shelburne Depot.

SHELBURNE DEPOT

Operational railroads required a host of outbuildings — sheds, garages, and shanties of all sorts. Foremost among railroad architectural curiosa is the station itself. From Ancient Rome and Greece came plans of temples and baths, and even way stations and whistle stops boasted fashionable waiting rooms and ticket offices with a baggage room close by.

Shelburne Depot, built in 1890 by Dr. W. Seward Webb, then President of the Rutland Railroad, is complete in every detail. The telegraphers key resounds through the Victorian structure which has been turned into a gallery of railroad mementos and artifacts. The station is the gift of Mr. Vanderbilt Webb and Mr. Cyril Jones to the Shelburne Museum.

Displayed inside are excursion broadsides and bills of lading as well as a remarkable collection of photographs. Railroad manuals and year books sit idly by as outside, the Baldwin engine # 220, her boiler stilled forever, waits for the engineer who will never grasp her throttle again.

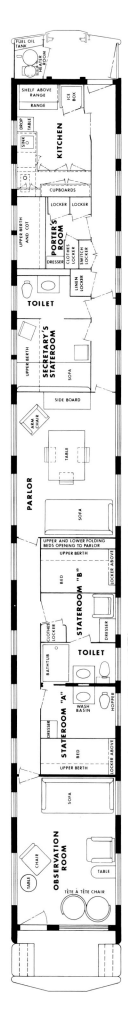

THE PRIVATE CAR "GRAND ISLE"

The railroads brought a new facet to an already kaleidoscopic American scene. The day of the great tycoon and industrial giant arrived, and with his new wealth came a desire for elegance and luxury. Victorian art acquiesced.

The Private Railroad Car provided the wealthy a plush and comfortable way to travel. Whole private trains hauled hosts and guests over the streaks of rust which crisscrossed the continent in every direction. It was a welcome escape from the passenger coaches where hawkers, miscreants and riff-raff could make a disaster of almost any journey.

The "Grand Isle" was built by the Wagner Palace Car Company about 1890 and was presented by the President of the Company, Dr. W. Seward Webb, to the Governor of Vermont, Edward C. Smith. With mahogany panelling refinished to mirror gloss, gleaming hardware, and velvets everywhere, "private varnish" was a symbol of the new rank.

THE
S.S. TICONDEROGA

Length	220'
Beam	57½'
Draft	11½'
Displacement	892 tons
Horsepower	1500
Top Speed	23 mph
Cruising Speed	17 mph
Capacity	1200 persons
Crew	28

The S.S. Ticonderoga started her career in 1906 in the shipyards at Shelburne Harbor on Lake Champlain. For 47 years, this steel-hulled sidewheeler cruised the length and breadth of Lake Champlain carrying passengers, freight, and even the automobiles which, in the end, did so much to bring about her forced retirement. By 1950, the aging steamboat was no longer a paying proposition and seemed destined to be broken up for its value as scrap metal. If it had not been for the vigorous action of a citizens' committee, led by Ralph Nading Hill of Burlington, the "Ti" would, today, be just a memory. Under the auspices of the Burlington Junior Chamber of Commerce and, later, the Shelburne Museum, the "Ti" remained afloat four more years as a tourist vessel. But the problems of maintaining the old boat through autumn hurricanes and winter snow and ice, of cleaning, repairing and licensing the ancient boilers, and of finding trained crewmen, proved a losing battle. The decision to move the "Ti" to the Shelburne Museum grounds seemed the best way to avert disaster and to preserve the boat for future generations.

97

Once the decision to move the "Ti" to Shelburne Museum had been made, the enormity of such an unprecedented operation became apparent. Engineering for the 9,250 foot overland journey was done by the firm of Merritt, Chapman and Scott of New York, while much of the actual work was handled by a subcontractor, the W. B. Hill Company of Tilton, New Hampshire. The plan, while simple in theory, was complex in execution. It called for floating the "Ti" to Shelburne Bay, a location less than two miles from the museum grounds. There a dike would be constructed around the "Ti" to form a basin 450 feet long. This would be flooded after the fashion of a canal lock to raise the "Ti" from lake level and float her forward over an immense carriage made of 64 railway wheels and designed to receive her hull. Once the water was withdrawn and the dike removed, the "Ti" could be winched to the museum grounds over the railroad tracks laid ahead in sections.

Plans for the move were predicated on the freezing weather and frozen ground so typical of Vermont winters. But unseasonably warm spells nearly caused disaster on two occasions. During the ticklish business of floating the "Ti" onto its carriage, the basin's earthen dike began springing leaks. At a time when the plans called for pumping water out to lower the hull into position, the leaks necessitated that water be pumped in to prevent the level from receding prematurely. In spite of the emergency, the "Ti" was brought to rest with its keel only ¼" from dead center on the cradle. Later on in the operation, while the "Ti" was moving over a stretch of low ground, an early thaw threatened to soften the frozen earth. There was a very real danger that the "Ti" might mire or even capsize. Only the valiant effort by the entire crew enabled crossing the critical terrain before the spring flooding which very nearly delayed completion of the move another year. On April 6, 1955, after an overland journey of 65 days, the S.S. Ticonderoga reached its newly constructed berth at Shelburne Museum.

The safe arrival at this last harbor marked the beginning of a new phase in the "Ti's" long career. Its water history far behind and its traveling days over, the "Ti" rests like an old veteran retired from active service, who, having outlived all the old comrades, is content to live on in quiet leisure, spending time with the youngsters and relating to them yarns and adventures of times long past.

The S.S. Ticonderoga in her permanent berth appears from a distance to be passing the Colchester Reef Lighthouse, just as she did daily for many years on Lake Champlain. Today the "Ti's" walls are hung with paintings, prints, broadsides, and photos — all depicting the heyday of the steam transportation era. Tourists still walk the "Ti's" decks and corridors, and as they look about, they find themselves cruising off on an excursion into maritime history.

Metamora, James Bard, 1859

Sidewheeler Josephine
Artist Unknown

Shelburne Harbor, Early 1920's

Recognizing her unique contribution to an understanding of our cultural heritage, the U.S. Department of the Interior, in 1963, declared the S.S. Ticonderoga a National Historic Landmark.

American Steamboat About 1820, Artist Unknown

S.S. Ticonderoga Engine Room

Nelly Baker, James Bard

L. L. McAllister

THE WEBB GALLERY

As early as 1957, Electra Webb saw the need for an art gallery as a necessary adjunct to her collection of Americana. Paintings and pieces of furniture, whose numbers had long exceeded the museum's capacity for display, found a permanent home when the Webb Gallery was first opened to the public in 1960. The canvases on exhibit cover a wide range of variety from the "primitive" attempts of anonymous painters to the sophisticated academic works of America's most important artists, and as a collection, they span three centuries of American life.

Greeting visitors at the gallery entrance stands the ten-foot tall carved pine figure of Justice which once surmounted the courthouse at Barnstable, Massachusetts. Andrew Wyeth's *Soaring* is visible through the doorway in the room beyond.

Among the many examples of early American furniture, exhibited in the gallery, is this Hepplewhite chest of drawers, interesting for its marble top carved with the records of births and deaths of a Connecticut family. Above the chest hangs a portrait of *Red Jacket,* Chief of the Senecas, painted on a wood panel by an unknown artist.

More than any other of the museum's buildings, the Webb Gallery was a joint effort by husband and wife. Electra Webb excelled in design and selection and attended to the innumerable details requiring the sensitivity of a woman's touch, while her husband, Watson, financed acquisition of a major portion of the collection. But J. Watson Webb made contributions to the Shelburne Museum which were far more basic. It was he who introduced Electra to the Vermont landscape and he who developed in his wife a love for early American architecture. It was the goal of preserving his own family's carriage collection that brought the museum into existence, and at a pivotal point in the museum's development, it was Watson who proposed the moving of the Vergennes Schoolhouse to the museum grounds, the museum's first major step in building relocation and reconstruction. Throughout the often trying episodes of Shelburne Museum's growth, J. Watson Webb remained a continuing source of inspiration and encouragement to his wife. The Webb Gallery was their last project together, for both Watson and Electra passed away in 1960, the year of the gallery's opening.

The portrait, by George C. Munzig, shows Lila Vanderbilt Webb and son, J. Watson Webb, in the year 1889. It was Watson's father, Dr. William Seward Webb, who established the family's summer home at Shelburne.

J. Watson Webb
as he appeared in 1957

103

Americans . . .

Rev. W. Lawson
and *Nancy Lawson*
by William
Matthew Prior

Aunt Dolly (Mrs. Oliver Dickenson)
Attributed to Erastus Salisbury Field

Selling Corn
by George H. Durrie

Susan Smith Elmer and *Erastus Elmer* by Edwin Romanzo Elmer

The American Country Store
by A. B. Frost

*Gentleman of the
Brewer Family*
by William Jennys

Miss Jay
by Samuel F. B. Morse

Country Connoisseurs by Johannas Adam Simon Oertel

Jane Henrietta Russell
by Joseph Whiting Stock

... and the America they saw

View of Baltimore
by Fitz Hugh Lane

Niagara Falls
by Edmund C. Coates

House at Hoboken — 1854
by Capt. L. Luthy

Suffragettes Taking the
Constitution for a Sleigh Ride
Unknown Artist

Abandoned Farmhouse, Suffield, Connecticut
by Asa Cheffetz

Stone House at Larrabees Point
on Lake Champlain
by John George Brown

Conestoga Wagon
by Thomas Birch

The Falls at Vergennes, Vermont
by S. H. Washburn

Montpelier Station
Unknown Artist

House in the Trees
by Luigi Lucioni

THE SAWYER'S CABIN

Betsy Thrasher, The Artistic Alliance

During its search for clapboarding, the museum discovered such a cabin in Charlotte, Vermont. The square-hewn logs, painstakingly dovetailed at each corner, had been preserved by the sheathing of a succeeding age. Fashioned with broad axe and adze, these one-room havens boasted the most rudimentary furnishings, often with the earth itself for a floor.

The need for beams and masts for English ships greatly contributed to the settlement of northwestern Vermont, for settlers were quick to see the opportunity for commercial ventures, particularly the lumber trade. The forests provided the much-needed timber, and Lake Champlain and the Richelieu River provided a natural avenue for rafting it north to Montreal. From these same forests came the logs which sheltered the transient woodcutters. Although frame houses have always been predominate in New England, log cabins were built as temporary structures in the northwestern part.

THE UP AND DOWN SAWMILL

New settlers made additional demands of the American forest. Homes and barns, bridges, boats and wagons — the need for lumber was everywhere. It was as pressing as it was immense. When sawmilling replaced the pit saw technique, the machinery, which cut boards and planking, was, itself, made of wooden parts as the South Royalton, Vermont, sawmill testifies.

Here, water power has been harnessed to move a frame saw up and down, using an eccentric to create the alternating strokes. An idler at the top prevents excessive vibration of the saw and at the same time permits the saw to be adjusted to the density of the wood.

A log, riding the cog-toothed carriage, is fed into the blade by a friction drive which uses the same power source as the saw. This drive mechanism is a notable feature of the mill. Slowly, but effectively, this creaking, groaning "menagerie of wheels" manages to wrest a board from the stoutest log.

a. Eccentric
b. Idler
c. Cog-toothed Carriage
d. Friction Drive

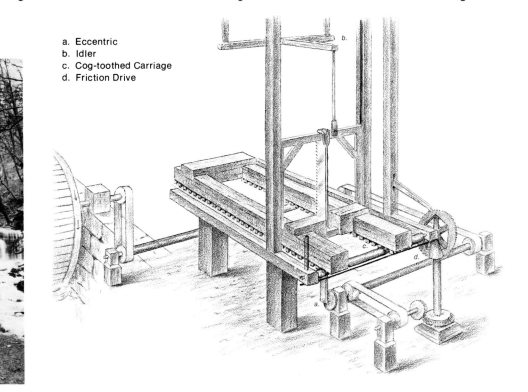

THE BEACH LODGE AND GALLERY

What rustic picture could be more appealing than a remote log cabin set in a snow-covered glade and pressed close by rocky ledges and silent evergreens! Indeed, this is the scene presented by Shelburne Museum's Beach Lodge and Gallery, two rough-hewn structures whose ancient timber and forest surroundings suggest the fastness of a north woods retreat. The buildings house the collections of North American big game trophies and related works of art and craftsmanship donated to Shelburne Museum by Marie and William Beach of Great Neck, Long Island, and collected by them during lifetimes of outdoor adventure. The trophies include such species as the Rocky Mountain goat, Alaskan moose, elk, Alaskan brown bear, caribou, and big horn sheep, just to name a few. The paintings on display in the Beach Gallery add depth to the collection and succeed in relating the story of the American outdoorsman, the animals he has hunted and the landscape he has loved.

Racquette Lake
by Arthur Fitzwilliam Tait

A number of the paintings on exhibit in the Beach Gallery are of historical interest. The large canvas on the left, *Farthest North* by Albert Operti, depicts the American arctic expedition of 1882. To its right hang examples of the work of Carl Rungius, the noted hunter and wildlife painter.

Unexpected Shot by Frederic Remington

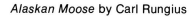
Alaskan Moose by Carl Rungius

Capt. Parker
by Arthur Fitzwilliam Tait

Grouse in Flight
by Archibald Thorburn

Trapper in the Wilderness by Sidney Laurence

Complementing the mellow golden log interior of the Beach Lodge are numerous Indian artifacts with their brightly colored patterns and fascinating designs. The fringed cape hanging between the two beds is typical of the work of the Chilkat Indians of the Pacific Northwest.

THE CIRCUS PARADE

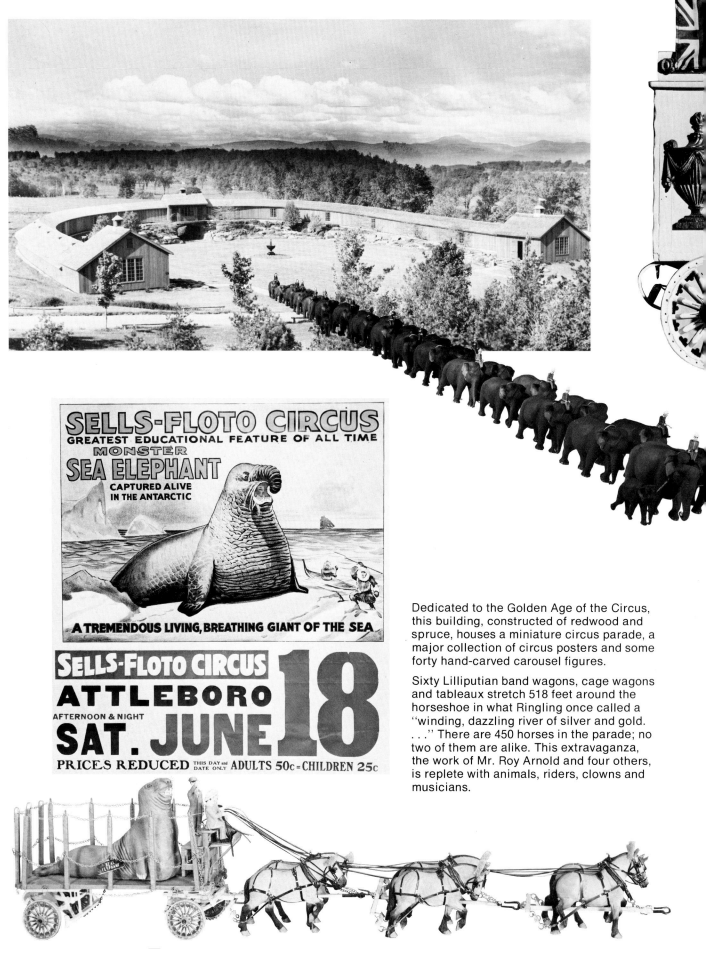

Dedicated to the Golden Age of the Circus, this building, constructed of redwood and spruce, houses a miniature circus parade, a major collection of circus posters and some forty hand-carved carousel figures.

Sixty Lilliputian band wagons, cage wagons and tableaux stretch 518 feet around the horseshoe in what Ringling once called a "winding, dazzling river of silver and gold. . . ." There are 450 horses in the parade; no two of them are alike. This extravaganza, the work of Mr. Roy Arnold and four others, is replete with animals, riders, clowns and musicians.

Also displayed here is a panorama of "billboard art"—a collection of advertising lithographs which chronicle the history of the American circus. All of the major road shows are represented in the poster collection—a mixture of ballyhoo and art which stirs the nostalgic memories of those who remember the days of the street parade.

Photos by C. Robert Callahan and Einars J. Mengis

113

ELECTRA HAVEMEYER WEBB MEMORIAL BUILDING

Electra Havemeyer Webb (1888-1960)
Portrait by Elizabeth Shoumatoff

The original entrance hall of the
740 Park Avenue apartment of
Mr. and Mrs. J. Watson Webb

Mr. and Mrs. Henry O. Havemeyer

114

Electra Havemeyer was the second daughter and youngest child of Henry Osborne Havemeyer and Louisine Waldron Elder. From these two she acquired her wide knowledge of art, as well as her zest for collecting. The Havemeyers traveled abroad many times in their search for art, and under the guidance of the artist Mary Cassatt, they assembled a collection renowned for its diversity as well as its daring.

Although Electra's collecting interests took a different turn than that of her parents, it was her intention to bring to Shelburne a building which would be a memorial to Mr. and Mrs. Havemeyer and house her portion of their European art and sculpture.

Mr. and Mrs. Webb died within eight months of each other in 1960. Their children then decided to bring their mother's idea to a reality and construct a building which would house the Havemeyer art in appropriate settings. For this, nothing more suitable recommended itself than their apartment at 740 Park Avenue in New York. It was then that a seven-year venture began.

Six rooms were removed from the apartment and brought, in their entirety, to Shelburne. They were reconstructed and refurbished; no detail of the interiors being untended to or overlooked. So exact was the result that the rooms appear to the visitor as if Mr. and Mrs. Webb had just stepped out for a minute.

This beautiful Greek revival-type building, overlooking Shelburne Museum was opened to the public in 1967, a memorial to Electra H. Webb and her husband, J. Watson Webb.

Mr. and Mrs. Webb lived at 740 Park Avenue for more than thirty years, and during that time filled seventeen rooms with beautiful appointments and objets d'art. Fine English panelling and antique furniture shared a compatible world with Rembrandt, Degas, Corot, Manet and other artists.

Because of the exquisite blending of old world treasures, the apartment achieved a quiet elegance, charm and warmth. It was this "world apart" that Mrs. Webb felt should be preserved and which eventually came to Vermont and to Shelburne Museum.

Largest of the six rooms which were moved to the museum is the *Living Room*. Its antique panelling dates from the second quarter of the Eighteenth Century and was taken from Cocken Hall in County Durham. Dominating the room are two paintings by Rembrandt van Rijn, *Man in a Broad-Brimmed Hat* (1643) and *The Treasurer* (1632). The furnishings are Queen Anne and Chippendale, some upholstered in needlepoint. Over the mantel hangs the painting, *Two Ballet Girls,* by Edgar Degas. The rug is Chinese and all hand tied.

With panels and mouldings of English leather, the *Library* is an admirable creation. The warm brown tones and re-flecting light patterns enhance the truly noble character of the room. Mr. and Mrs. Webb shared a great love for hunting, and this room reflects that mutual interest, as the walls are hung with hunt paintings. Most notable of these is Ben Marshall's *Huntsman and Hounds* (1802) which hangs above the fireplace. Several of Antoine-Louis Barye's remarkable bronze animals occupy vari-ous niches over the book cases. The chairs and sofas are covered with old printed linen which lends an air of quiet informality to the room, and the rug is brown velvet.

The *Dining Room* is panelled with horizontal sheathing taken from a home in Argyle Place, Westminster, London, and dates about 1750. A large Palladian window in the south wall admits both morning and afternoon sunlight which adds a beautiful luster to the antique Chippendale table, as well as the light amber panelling. This window is flanked by a pair of Adams Balustre-Form marble and bronze candelabra with beaded prisms and a Wedgewood medallion. In addition to a rare set of Chippendale ribbon-back chairs, upholstered in brown leather, the room is furnished with an American Hepplewhite Serpentine Chest and an Adams carved mahogany sideboard with fluted apron and swag motif supports. A collection of Tanagra figurines, paintings by Monet, and pieces of Wedgewood and Leeds Pottery complete the decor.

The panelling in *Mr. Webb's Bedroom* is English pine
and comes from a home in Stepney Causeway, London,
which dates about 1740. Mr. Webb was a superb horse-
man and a high goal polo player for a quarter of a century, and his great love of polo and fox hunting is reflected in the sporting prints and paintings in this room.
The furnishings are antique pieces of rather unpreten-
tious lines, and their rich mahogany is accented by the
lustrous golden brown interior panels and mouldings.
The side chairs are Chippendale, and a bible box stands
at the foot of the bed. Mr. Webb's desk returned to the
room as a gift of his grandson, Samuel B. Webb, Jr., to
whom Mrs. Webb had given it.

The Green Room is an exquisitely proportioned room, with furnishings and appointments of the Louis XV Period. The panelling comes from a house on Redcliffe Parade, Bristol, England, and dates from the third to the last quarter of the Eighteenth Century. A delicate Louis XV French Provincial Fruitwood desk provides an appropriate stage for Monet's *Bridge Over the Thames.* A Beechwood Duchesse chair, upholstered in green cut velvet, and a Louis XV Fruitwood Fauteuil, in white embroidered silk damask, stand on either side of the fireplace, over which there is a beautiful Acajou and Gilt Mantel Mirror. A painting by Robert Noir, *Portrait of Two Children,* hangs to the right of the fireplace and a lovely little pastel by Whistler sits upon the desk between two Louis XVI urn-shaped candlesticks.

Mrs. Webb's Bedroom is antique boiserie which was removed from Wenvoe Castle, Glamorgan, and dates around 1775. From above the fireplace, the *Princesa de La Paz,* attributed to Goya (1746-1828), serenely watches the approaching visitor, and over Mrs. Webb's desk is a portrait of her mother, Mrs. Henry O. Havemeyer, done by Mary Cassatt. Lacquered and decorated French Provincial furniture, with occasional American pieces, create a soft and very feminine atmosphere. A beautiful crewel spread covers the bed, while the beige silk curtains and beige rug blend with the background of the spread and with the fabric-covered end boards of the bed.

Among four paintings by Edgar Degas which are exhibited in the Memorial Building, his *Danseuse à La Barre*, was chosen by Mrs. Webb to be hung over the dressing table in her bedroom.

In 1929, Mrs. Henry O. Havemeyer bequeathed her collection of art to the Metropolitan Museum of Art. Believing there were others who were as interested and intelligent in art as she was, she gave the gift without restriction, and this enabled that museum "to rank with the great," since the Havemeyer collection could then be used to fill out sparser areas and several incomplete collections. She counseled her children to give the choicest items to the museum, even to surrendering their own claims if she had overlooked the importance of one or another piece. Because of the generosity of the children, Mrs. P. H. B. Frelinghuysen, Mr. Horace Havemeyer, and Mrs. J. Watson Webb, the bequest swelled from 142 to 1,967 superb works of art.

There still remained some of the finest art in America in her children's own homes, and it is a portion of this which now graces the beautiful interiors of the Electra Havemeyer Webb Memorial Building.

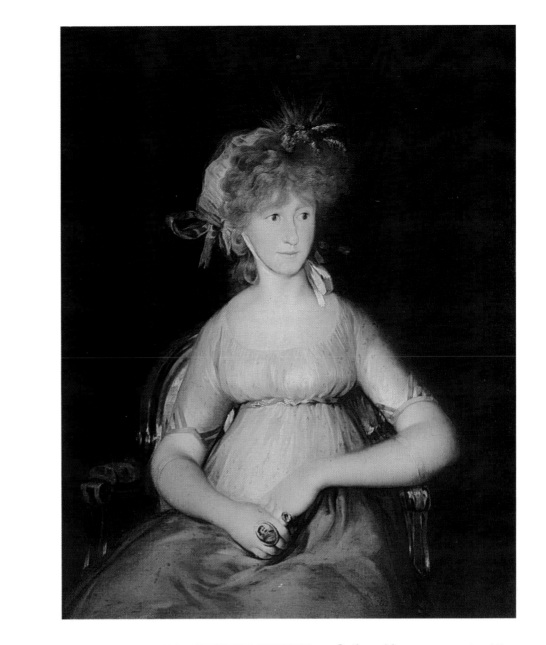

Gathered from many parts of Europe, the variegated collection included not only the recognized schools of painting and their masters, but also what was, at that time, avant-garde, the modern Impressionists like Manet, Courbet and Corot. Although aghast at the desires and interests of their daughter, Electra, who pursued American antiques and art with a fervor equalling theirs, Mr. and Mrs. Havemeyer provided the atmosphere and surroundings that tempered choices of their daughter. That, too, is a priceless legacy.

(Above left, opposite page) Huntsman and Hounds, Ben Marshall, 1802

(Below left, opposite page) Man in a Broad-Brimmed Hat, Rembrandt van Rijn, 1643

(Center) Mrs. Henry O. Havemeyer, Mary Cassatt, 1899

(Above right) Princesa de la Paz, attributed to Francesco Goya

(Left) Blue Venice, Edouard Manet, 1875

With meticulous care and infinite patience, the museum workmen brought to life the plans and paper work of designers and of architect William Wilson. *The Circular Staircase,* descending through three stories, will always remain a tribute to their craftsmanship and artistry. Tucked behind this staircase is a small tea room, and beside its doorway hang Courbet's *Still Life — Fruit* and Manet's *Blue Venice.*

Executed with consummate taste and talent, the Memorial Building justifiably takes its place among the architectural Americana at Shelburne, a tribute to Mr. and Mrs. J. Watson Webb and to all who made their dream a reality.

THE OGDEN M. PLEISSNER BUILDING

Ogden M. Pleissner (1905-1983), the dean of American sporting artists, was a superbly talented landscape painter. Mr. Pleissner was a member and former president of the National Academy of Design; his work is represented in the collections of some 65 museums, including in addition to Shelburne, the Metropolitan, Brooklyn and Philadelphia Museums of Art. Mr. Pleissner is best known for his "sporting art", beautiful renderings, primarily in watercolor, of hunting and fishing scenes: salmon rivers, trout streams, upland bird covers and duck marshes. However, despite his success with such scenes, Mr. Pleissner considered himself not a sporting artist but rather "a landscape painter, a painter of landscapes who also likes to hunt and fish."

Ogden Pleissner was born in Brooklyn and studied at the Art Students League in New York. As a correspondent for the Army Airforce in WWII, his watercolors of the Aleutians, England and France appeared regularly in Life magazine. Mr. Pleissner returned to Europe once a year for more than thirty years to paint landscapes and to enjoy hunting and fishing in England and Scotland. He was a Trustee of the Shelburne Museum for twenty years.

The Ogden Pleissner building was erected in 1985-86 with funds donated by Mr. Pleissner's widow, Marion and his oldest friend, Samuel B. Webb, Sr. The building includes a large gallery which displays watercolors, oils and sketches by Mr. Pleissner chosen from the large collection of his works in the Museum's collection. In addition, there is a recreation of the artist's Manchester, Vermont studio—a large, sunny room filled with American Indian artifacts, decoys and other favorite objects as well as canvasses, paints, brushes and easels.

Blue Boat on the St. Anne, 1958

The Round Barn in its original site, E. Passumpsic, Vermont

THE ROUND BARN

Built in East Passumpsic, Vermont in 1901 by Fred "Silo" Quimby, a local carpenter with a reputation for building ringed silos, the Round Barn was moved to Shelburne in 1985-86. The unusual barn was taken apart plank by plank and beam by beam. It was moved and reconstructed at the Museum by Graton and Sons of Ashland, New Hampshire, specialists in the moving of covered bridges. The 9000 lb center silo was airlifted across Vermont by skycrane helicopter in March 1986 and set safely into the center of the partially reconstructed barn. Moving the silo by air was the only way to preserve the tightly constructed structure intact. The airlift was made possible by grants from United Technologies Corporation and two of its operating units, Pratt and Whitney and Sikorsky.

The three story barn, which is built around a center silo, is 60′ tall and 80′ in diameter. Its dramatic cathedral-like upper floor served as the hay mow. The middle or dairy floor had ties for 60 cows facing in toward the circular feed trough, an arrangement which greatly reduced feeding time. Manure fell through trap doors to the basement. The entire pit was built with long ceiling timbers and no support posts to allow the farmer to drive his horse team and spreader around the basement to get into position under the manure chutes.

Round barns have always fascinated travelers and served as important rural landmarks. Had tractors not come along to revolutionize agriculture many more probably would have been built. Fewer than two dozen were put up in Vermont, however, and about 18 of them burned, collapsed or were too extensively modified or added onto for public interpretive use. The Round Barn at Shelburne is the best available example of this forgotten and fascinating architectural form.

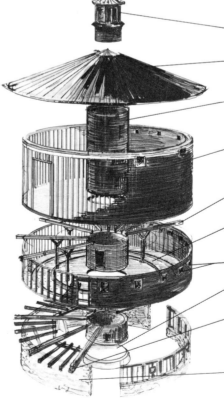

CUPOLA: This decorative cap to the building served as ventilation into the silo.

ROOF: Cedar shingles cover 8000 square feet. The barn is 80′ in diameter, 67′ from lightning rod to basement.

SILO: Structural core of the building. Primarily designed for corn storage but used mostly for hay silage. Top section is 29′ high and 20′ in diameter.

SHEATHING: Exterior skin has two thicknesses of ⅝″ pine planks bent and nailed to 2″ × 5″ vertical studs. Double layering prevented rain and snow from entering.

HAY FLOOR JOISTS: Beams carry full weight of hay above and anchor vertical supports for cattle stanchions.

DAIRY FLOOR: Main production section. Cattle were fed with hay from floor above while manure fell through opening to pit below.

WINDOWS: Large windows provided plenty of light and ventilation.

SILO BASE: Originally banded with steel compression rings, base later encased in concrete.

OVERSIZE FLOOR TIMBERS: Heavy beams and metal screw trusses allowed clear span. Absence of support posts made it possible to drive a team of horses and manure spreader into the basement for loading.

SIDE HILL FOUNDATION: Barns often were built on hillsides to allow walk-in grade access at all levels.

THE ELECTRA WEBB BOSTWICK GARDEN

Electra Webb Bostwick, the eldest child of Museum founders Mr. and Mrs. J. Watson Webb, surrounded herself with flowers throughout her life. She always maintained a beautiful garden at her home in Shelburne. She was also an accomplished artist; flowers picked from her garden were the subject of many of her canvases.

Mrs. Bostwick started painting at age eleven when she was in the sixth grade. When she was a young girl, Mrs. Bostwick's grandmother, Louisine W. Havemeyer, used to let her take portfolios of Degas' drawings and Mary Cassatt etchings home to copy. Mrs. Havemeyer also gave her Mary Cassatt's six-tier tray of French pastels with which to work. In later years Mrs. Bostwick feared that many of the colors had been used for hopscotch.

Mrs. Bostwick, who later studied with Archipenko and family friends Luigi Lucioni and Ogden Pleissner, had several solo shows of her work in New York. Being a very modest and private person, she was uncomfortable about showing her work in public and donated all the proceeds from these shows to charity. A number of Mrs. Bostwick's paintings of flowers are in the Shelburne Museum collection, including three which hang in her mother's bedroom in the Electra Havemeyer Webb Memorial Building.

The lovely Electra Webb Bostwick garden, planted with pansies, roses and other favorites of Mrs. Bostwick, was made possible by donations from family members and friends.

At the dedication of the Garden on August 6, 1986, Ralph Nading Hill remarked,

"We have all known a few people whose imprint upon the lives of those around them was so pronounced that we still feel their presence. Like her namesake, the founder of this museum, Electra Webb Bostwick was such a person.

Intelligent, shy, and sensitive, she was committed to her family and several households, her painting, and intimate circle of friends—in that order.

She was a perfectionist who demonstrated her lifetime quest for beauty in everything she did. Since she beheld beauty in all her relationships, she herself was the personification of it. She spared nothing for the wellbeing of her family and friends and for the enjoyment of those around her lavishly spent her energy on humorous running commentaries about the follies and foibles of this world.

…how particularly fitting that Electra's husband and children have created this beautiful place where her favorite flowers will always suggest the essence of her character to those who did not know her, and offer a fragrant and loving remembrance to those who did."

Electra Webb Bostwick, October 1949

Turtle Baby by Edith Parsons

Photograph by Eric Bessette

130

WE LIVE IN DEEDS, NOT YEARS:

In thoughts, not breaths:
In feelings, not in figures on a dial.
We should count time by heart-throbs.
He most lives who thinks most,
    feels the noblest, acts the best.

— Philip J. Bailey